# Carol Carnage

# Carol Carnage

Malicious Mishearings of Your Yuletide Favourites

Atlantic Books
London

First published in Great Britain in 2015 by Atlantic Books, an imprint of Atlantic Books Ltd.

10 9 8 7 6 5 4 3 2 1

A CIP catalogue record for this book is available from the British Library.

Hardback ISBN: 978 1 78239 785 4

Printed in Great Britain

Atlantic Books
An Imprint of Atlantic Books Ltd
Ormond House
26–27 Boswell Street
London
WC1N 3JZ

www.atlantic-books.co.uk

For Miss Jacqueline BOND, punatrice extraordinAIRE, and as EVER, with all my LOVE, for ANNA, FRED & ROSE

# GOD REST YE MERRY, GENTLEMEN

God rest ye merry, gentlemen,
  Let nothing you dismay,
For Jesus Christ, our Saviour,
  Was born upon this day,
To save us all from Satan's power,
  When we had gone astray,
O tidings of comfort and joy,
    Comfort and joy,
O tidings of comfort and joy.

# Got dressed yet, Mary? ...

# ... Gin till morn!

# Late Knifing-ewe display,

# Worst Porn ape on this tie,

(Sat on spar,)

# One We-ird gonk ashtray,

SOUVENIR of REIGATE

Happy Christmas from Auntie Mildred

# O-o-oh Thai dins (off) ...

# Kumquats and Joyce!

# O-oh Tidings of Co-omfort and Joy.

# In the Bleak Midwinter

In the bleak midwinter,
Frosty wind made moan,
Earth stood hard as iron,
Water like a stone;
Snow had fallen, snow on snow,
Snow on snow,
In the bleak midwinter,
Long ago.

What can I give Him,
Poor as I am?
If I were a shepherd,
I would bring a lamb;
If I were a wise man,
I would do my part;
What I can, I give Him —
Give my heart.

# Ian the Greek, mid-wine tour.

# Throws tea...

... *Wins!* ...

# ...Maids moan.

# Oaf, stewed...

# ...Howdah Siren,

# Waiter lurks (he's stoned);

# Snared fel-on...

... *Snood on Shmoe,*

# Schmoooooooozing shmoe,

I am the Greek, mid-wine tour,
Lo-onging to go.

HEM HEM

# Warty Canid, Gotham,

# Po-orous iamb.

# Offer war...

... *Ash-heap hoard,*

# Eye-ward bling... alarm!

"Ever wash rabbis, man?"

# Wet-icon archive...

# Gi-ive us his heart !

# Once in Royal David's City

Once in Royal David's City,
Stood a lowly cattle shed,
Where a mother laid her baby,
In a manger for his bed.
Mary was that mother mild,
Jesus Christ her little child.

# Winching rural divots's shitty,

Stodge alone leaves cat all shed,

# Wow! Another leder baby.

# In a major Pharaoh's bod.

# Myrrhy wasp ...

... Fat mothy smiled,

# Cheeses riced ...

... her li-ittle child.

# DING DONG Merrily on HIGH

Ding dong merrily on high,
In heav'n the bells are ringing:
Ding dong! verily the sky,
Is riv'n with angel singing.
Gloria, Hosanna in excelsis!
Gloria, Hosanna in excelsis!

# DING DONG!...

... *Moral* **Leon** ...

50

# Those Heathens their balls are minging:

Dung Tongue! Vilely this guy,

# Is ruined by ungelled swinging.

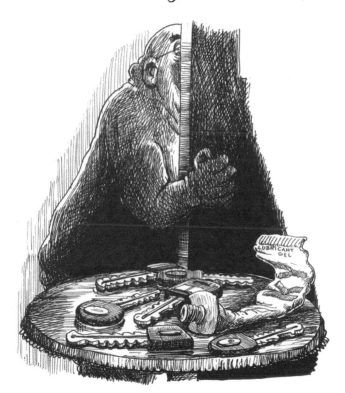

"Glo-o-o-o-o-o-o-o-o-o-o-o-o-o-o-
oria!"...

...Horse in an annex chases!

"Glo-o-o-o-o-o-o-o-o-o-o-o-o-o-o-o-o.
oria!!"...

...Hosed in an Onyx cha-a-alice!

# O Come, All Ye Faithful

O Come, All Ye Faithful,
Joyful and triumphant,
O come ye, O come ye to Bethlehem.
Come and behold Him,
Born the King of Angels;
O come, let us adore Him,
O come, let us adore Him,
O come, let us adore Him,
Christ the Lord.

# A Kümmelly Fi-i-ifa.

# Jail Forlorn Trium-virate.

61

# ...OaKu-u-um Yeti-i...

... Bear-r-r Phlegm.

# Common beheadings.

Bona Klingon angels;

E-Comm lout is a Tory,

# Elk Ham, lettuce adornment,

Orc cum litter's absor-or-or-orbent,

# "Chri-ist I'm bored!"